Power Rooms

Executive Offices
Corporate Lobbies
Conference Rooms

Photography by Jack D. Neith
Written by Oleta Neith

Schiffer Publishing Ltd

4880 Lower Valley Road Atglen, Pennsylvania 19310

Dedication

This book is dedicated to my wife, Oleta, who has assisted me throughout our lives together. Without her love and support, this book and the photography throughout it would not have been possible.

Disclaimer and Acknowledgments of Trademarks

Most of the items and products in this book may be covered by various copyrights, trademarks, and logotypes. Their use herein is for identification purposes only. All rights are reserved by their respective owners.

The text and products pictured in this book are from the collection of the author of this book, and its publisher. This book is not sponsored, endorsed or otherwise affiliated with any of the companies whose products are represented herein. This book is derived from the author's independent research.

All rights are reserved. No duplication or reproduction without the express written permission from the author or publisher.

Designed by John P. Cheek
Cover design by Bruce Waters
Type set in Futura XBlk BT/Zurich BT

ISBN: 978-0-7643-2920-3
Printed in China

Schiffer Books are available at special discounts for bulk purchases for sales promotions or premiums. Special editions, including personalized covers, corporate imprints, and excerpts can be created in large quantities for special needs. For more information contact the publisher.

Published by Schiffer Publishing Ltd.
4880 Lower Valley Road
Atglen, PA 19310
Phone: (610) 593-1777; Fax: (610) 593-2002
E-mail: Info@schifferbooks.com

For the largest selection of fine reference books on this and related subjects, please visit our web site at **www.schifferbooks.com**
We are always looking for people to write books on new and related subjects. If you have an idea for a book please contact us at the above address.

This book may be purchased from the publisher.
Include $3.95 for shipping.
Please try your bookstore first.
You may write for a free catalog.

In Europe, Schiffer books are distributed by
Bushwood Books
6 Marksbury Ave.
Kew Gardens
Surrey TW9 4JF England
Phone: 44 (0) 20 8392-8585; Fax: 44 (0) 20 8392-9876
E-mail: info@bushwoodbooks.co.uk
Website: www.bushwoodbooks.co.uk
Free postage in the U.K., Europe; air mail at cost.

Contents

Introduction

This book has developed over twenty-five years of interior photography in the "power rooms" of corporate America. I worked with architects, interior designers, manufactures, and public relation firms on assignments throughout the United States. This cross-section of corporate designs shows the excesses of the 1980s, which produced glamour and glitz, and the creative edge of designers with limited budgets in the 1990s to the present day. The uses of different materials and designs make each environment unique. Color and texture play an important function. Impressive views, lighting, and structural containment all add to the ambience of the environment. The subtle sense of contrast and harmony of natural light that plays with interior landscaping makes an impact upon sophisticated design.

Some photographs depict simple design utilizing creativity, color, and function as their inspiration. Others incorporate bold statements in design elements to create a memorable design. The elegance of woods, polished marbles, and other surfaces create the illusion of importance. The accent lighting used in many of the spaces adds drama to the designs.

Chapter 1
Atriums, Lobbies and Reception Areas

Books are knowledge. Knowledge is power. Turn the pages and enter our world of Power Rooms.

Wooden arches caress steel beams creating a spacious and elegant lobby.

Inspired by America's majestic redwood forests, the designer fills this lobby with beautiful wood structures that grow to the ceiling.

The seating area induces calm and solitude amongst the "tree" lined space.

Corner detail of the intricate column work in a modern office space.

The power of nature is depicted
through this winding wood path
through a symbolic thicket of trees.

Strong white columns encircle this entrance with the world depicted in marble on the floor. The hallway invites visitors with beautifully illuminated red walls.

Cove lighting enhances this comfortably designed lobby with ample views of conversational artwork. Hues of blue and cream create comfort with a sleek and crisp design.

Decorative wood patterns in the floor direct visitors to a posh seating area in this art filled lobby.

Detailed parquet wood resembles a hand loomed carpet making this a very special interior environment.

Primitive inspired sculpture and modern art add to the clean modern lines of this space.

The power of red embodies this lobby seating area with similar designs in both the floor and wall art.

Sensuous sunlight glistens onto the neutral textures in this impeccably adorned lobby. Organic shapes in the carpet along with decorative greenery bring the outdoors in.

Symmetry of burgundy chairs, light fixtures and windows are a captivating view in this ample lobby.

Traditionally inspired seating with green and beige hues dominate this column bordered lobby.

13

Empowering black stairs carry the eye upward to the second floor through the teardrop shaped ceiling cove.

A wall of glass allows for full vision of this dynamic curvaceous space.

Contrasting white and black appointments create depth and illusion to this hallway.

Strong wooden hues encompass this empowered
lobby with a view of the exquisite boardroom.

Curving walls and neutral browns are the focal points of this lobby. Priceless art adds beauty and visual interest to the expansive receptionist wall.

This huge lobby space is centered by deep red chairs on a blue grey carpet.

Crisp and clean, white and beige, this lobby creates strong contrasting hues against the beautiful wood appointments.

18

A crystalline glass block wall creates mystery and drama in this upscale lobby.

Retro chairs and rust colored hues surround this comfortable lobby space.

19

The organic curves of the reception desk and ceiling cove induce warmth and comfort in this neutrally colored lobby.

Richly hued columns border this lobby with accents of deep green marble.

Sparkling glass and brass create an endless illusion to this stairway to heaven. This high rise lobby is an endless vision of seamless clarity above the hustle and bustle of the city below.

Triangles and glass continue to intertwine in this opulent lobby. Artwork and chairs in pleasing hues of blue compliment the natural colors of the sky and landscape views.

Opposing page:
A breathless view of sunset is seen from this angled wall of glass. An enormous oriental carpet anchors the comfortable seating area as the repetition of triangles and sharp points dominate the space.

Primary blue and secondary green encompasses this stately lobby with marbled Corinthian columns and intricately detailed chandeliers.

A feeling of outdoors is created with the use of deep green marble on a neutral backdrop. Natural foliage further enhances the natural ambiance.

The pastel painting creates calm in this crisp bright area, which is anchored at the end with bright scarlet chairs.

Crimson stairs and contrasting bright green foliage add to the dramatic feeling of this contemporary lobby. Chrome columns and Italian marble floors complete the high tech interior.

25

Contemporary elegance exudes this lobby with black leather chairs and blue accent tables with chrome feet.

Opposing Page:
Slate blue seating and landscape paintings create
comfort and serenity in this clean design.

The elegance of symmetry is captured in this timeless design.

Shiny marble covers the floor and reception desk complimenting the pastel colored seats and greenery.

Shiny Italian marble compliments the rich wood panels in this elevator lobby.

Opposing page:
Expansive and spacious, the Italian marble creates a sea of elegance surrounding the reception desk and leading to the pristine white staircase with contrasting black railings. The reddish hue of the wood desk, banister and doors ties in nicely with the marble.

Diamond shaped medallions of marble on the floor lead to the upscale lobby framed by tall white columns and accented with an iridescent blue wall clock.

A sea of white marble and creamy white walls and ceiling act as a painter's backdrop to this symmetrically polished lobby.

Geometric angles in neutral hues envelope this contemporary view.

Clean and bright, this lobby has timeless appeal. Small diamond shapes in the marble floor follow the basic theme of this design.

This elevator lobby is enhanced by the large diamond marble floor design with strong color contrast of black, white, and red.

Contemporary beauty abounds in this lobby with a modern spiral staircase accented in glimmering brass.

Open and bright, this lobby provides comfortable seating amidst primaries in crimson and navy hues.

The outdoors are brought in with this serene setting of trees, foliage, and waterfall.

The central focal point of this design is captured by a circular floor design in contrasting black and white marble. Majestic trees and other tropical plants complete the setting.

The unique diamond marble floor design creates movement in this high tech contemporary space. Chrome and leather seating is complimented by exquisite artwork and a rare sculpture adorns the interior rock garden.

Detail of the serene rock garden adorned with unique sculptures borders the hallway leading to private offices.

Straightforward and contemporary, this lobby has powerful blue accents with a glass enclosed view.

Shiny marble, glass, chrome, and glass block are the main elements in this dramatically designed space with strong angles and points at every turn.

Contrasting green marble and reddish brown wood bring this lobby alive with color.

37

Contemporary angles and colors blend nicely in this elegant environment.

The indoor landscaping and the natural marble floor give you the feeling of sitting in a park while being indoors.

Looking down from the second floor into the main atrium this space is illuminated by a double row of skylights.

Looking down the contemporary staircase one can appreciate the vast sea of marble below, which leads to the glass encased exit doors.

Majestic symmetry envelops this contemporary main floor atrium with perfectly polished marble floors, dramatic skylights, and a centralized chrome staircase.

The tall green foliage sharply cuts into the crisp sterility created by white walls and shiny marble floors in this view of back to back conference rooms.

The diamond design enhanced by neutral hues in an art deco design accentuates this elegant elevator lobby.

Creative attention to detail in the wood trim in the ceiling and around the simulated skylights adds a feeling of nostalgia to this unique design.

Bright hues of orange, purple, and blue give a whimsical feeling to this seating space. The addition of ample foliage gives the impression of an outdoor park area in the comfort of the indoors.

This detail with a triangular focus is further illuminated by the skylights above.

Large scale artwork behind
the reception desk greets
visitors as they enter this
law firm.

This intimate seating is accented by
table lamps and a view to the outdoors,
which gives a feeling of home in a
public space.

Decorative tile work and an expansive sculpture dominate this multi level atrium.

Carpet that resembles tile encompasses the upstairs reception area in soothing sage green tones that compliments the earthy tones of the brick and tile work.

This lobby boasts plush velvet seating anchored by a crystalline marble floor in front of the elegant wooden reception desk.

Opposing page:
Curving glass walls encased in brass greet
visitors as they enter this lobby. A circular
design is created by the marble design
of the floor, the handles on the doors, the
niche displaying a sculpture, the curve of
the reception desk and sofa with the light
fixture above.

The Southwest lives in this lobby of
turquoise colored sofas, terra cotta
floor tiles, and white washed wood
wall panels. The cacti and succulents
along with the pottery accents and
wall art further add to this comfortable
design.

Pastel Southwestern inspired hues
paint a portrait of comfort and
serenity in this view of the lobby.

Neutral colors create a strong impact with concentric circles in this truly elegant lobby.

48

This detailed view of a keystone embellishes the archway.

The corridor leading to the reception area displays strong elements of symmetric design with marble wall panels and mirrored artwork.

Festive colors enhance this large atrium space. Tall trees and decorative foliage give the feeling of being in a beautiful outdoor park. The table lamps add to the ambiance by mimicking the shape of street lamps.

The feeling of being outdoors is also created by the carpet colors of brick to the left and right of the seating area with decorative lavender in between. Large paintings and wall coverings in green complete this indoor park scene.

The contrast of the greenery with the height of the atrium and the exterior view enhances this lobby.

Prominent skylights in a circular design encompass this comfortable seating area in the main lobby of a school.

Opposing page:
Angular and sleek, this contemporary design is softened by the strategic placement of burgundy leather seats and natural green plants.

Opposing page:
Subdued lighting with a darkened
curving hallway creates mystery and
a feeling of romance in this intimate
public setting.

Rich burgundy contrasts and
compliments the green hue of the
glass and natural plants in this
intimate lobby.

Bright yellow chrysanthemums catch
one's eye in this symmetrical lobby
design. Neutral walls and floor add to the
contrast created by the reception desk
and prominent columns.

54

Larger than life artwork on the wall produces drama and excitement in this lobby.

Tambour ceiling panels in exquisite warm wood add decorative dimension to this space.

CSC PARTNERS

Tranquil sea blue carpet surrounds this clean, crisp lobby.

Suave and sophisticated best describes this fashion designer's lobby in subdued shades of gray and pink.

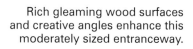

Rich gleaming wood surfaces and creative angles enhance this moderately sized entranceway.

58

Chromatic hues of grayish purple and turquoise blend nicely in this view. Symmetry is perceived from the seating area through to the conference room.

Glass walls enhance this capacious lobby as nature's blues and greens anchor the fixtures within the structure.

59

Right:
Powerful symmetry and circular design encase this lobby with colorful columns and a lustrous blue reception desk. Dramatic lighting and prominent marble accents complete the ambiance.

Far right:
Imaginative use of color and texture form an elegant and striking lobby.

Sharp angles and muted hues embody this reception area.

Traditional furnishings in subtle hues create a comfortable setting in this moderately sized lobby.

Cherry red chairs produce colorful excitement in this white, bright reception area.

Angles and light, polished
surfaces and symmetrical color
panels form an unforgettable
impression in this unique lobby.

An endless wall of radiant glass block surrounds a delicate purple and blue carpet amongst inviting chairs and vivid blue topped tables.

A prominent skylight adds to the luminosity of glass block in a comfortable setting.

64

The elements of nature depicted in the large landscape painting work in harmony with the greenery and blue hues used to create this lobby.

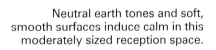

Neutral earth tones and soft, smooth surfaces induce calm in this moderately sized reception space.

Quiet and intimate, sea shades of blue and green blend well in this corporate environment.

Neutral colored walls and floor coverings surround the intense splash of color inherent in the lush leather sofa and chairs.

A bare bones ceiling is countered with smooth sleek interior design including a touch of whimsy with the framed window panel hanging above the hallway.

Strong crimson chair seats produce contrast and intensity in this otherwise neutral gray environment.

Cerulean blue carpet and peach colored chairs enhance this contemporary lobby.

High tech drama produces a
strong punch with neutral grays
and clean white hues.

An expansive lobby has intimate seating with a blending of cream and beige neutrals highlighted with strong red chairs.

Angular wall art and a splash of vivid red color brings this conference room to life.

Toned down values of gray and black dominant this comfortable seating area.

This expansive lobby area provides ample seating for many visitors while it includes a humorous touch with a full sized, functioning red telephone booth.

Art Deco inspired seating is complimented by vividly colored wall art and pleasingly displayed purple irises.

Earth tones compliment the fashion and function of this large commercial space.

Crisp and clean, neutral beiges form a comfortable setting in this corporate lobby.

Structural angles, dramatic lighting, and the use of powerful hues in red, purple, green, and black make a stunning statement in this ultra creative visual haven.

Sensual furniture shapes are complimented by an outstanding use of color. Fanciful design elements further enhance this contemporary masterpiece that creates an intimate setting in a public space.

74   Elegance and richness abound in this marble clad reception area. A circular desk adds interest and function to a highly polished façade.

Creative marble floor designs lead to a winding staircase complimented by the natural earth tones of glistening wood accoutrements.

Calming neutral colors surround the comfortable inviting chairs in this corporate lobby.

Domed lights illuminate the upstairs
seating area in neutral earth shades.

The power of angles and textures resonates in this sleek office interior.

Chapter 2
Executive Offices

Opposing page:
A breathtaking skyline view compliments the form and function of this spectacular space. Rich earth tones blend well with the use of geometric shapes.

Subdued neutral hues of the walls and floor creates an elegant and comfortable office. The structurally impressive window design allows for a sparkling illumination of natural sunlight.

Neutral grays compliment the reddish saturation of natural wood in this contemporary and comfortable office.

Richly hued wood paneling contrasts the use of neutrals adding visual stimulation to this private office.

Comfort abounds in this visitor friendly office that provides ample seating on luxurious leather sofas.

The green surface of the desk is a focal color point to this otherwise neutrally appointed office.

Fashionable expansive artwork and comfortable seating enhance this office that has it all, including a small conference table within the same room.

Large interior windows create an illusion of greater space in this modestly sized office.

An elegant four person desk unit lends functionality to this corner office.

Splashes of red chair cushions enliven this otherwise neutrally colored environment.

Deep powerful blues contrast nicely with the blond furniture in this contemporary design.

A functional desk return adds additional work space to this modest sized office.

Deep burgundy carpet and rich blue chairs add to the masculine feel of this private office.

Designed for a busy executive, this office boasts a conference table as well as scenic window views.

This huge office is adorned with an elegant granite topped conference table and an additional seating area to accommodate the most discerning visitors.

Traditional in design, this office
lends comfort with a window view.

Primitive inspired sculpture and earthenware adorn
this contemporary office with the added visual interest
created with a splash of modernism in the glass wall
partition and brilliant blue artwork.

Modern art adds playfulness to this contemporary space.

Crimson chairs and accessories contrast well with the neutrals in this office, which is lit with streamlined and efficient light fixtures.

Opposing page:
The serenity of the outdoors emerges within this office as slate blue and cerulean swirl about the room with accents of luscious green foliage.

An elegant oak wall unit beautifully accents the desk in this quaint masculine space.

Hunter green walls and floor form an exquisite backdrop for the decorative artwork and comfortable seating.

Textured green wall covering compliments the decorative carpet in this otherwise wood encased office. A large fireplace finishes the homey comfort of this elegant room.

A floral upholstered chair adds a touch of feminine delight to this very functional office with an expansive wall unit.

Modern desk design and ergonomic chairs produce a comfortable work station.

Comforting shades of blue abound in this contemporary office space.

Practical in size, this office allows for small conferences as well as private appointments.

Opposing page:
Light and airy, this office exudes elegance and comfort with subtle red and burgundy seating within an envelope of creamy textures of the walls and carpet.

Brilliant brown carpet anchors the elements in this productive office.

Lacquered black furniture and intense subdued blues appear dramatic in this monochromatic setting.

Colorful and stunning modern art catapults this contemporary office into a league by itself.

96

Deep blue carpet and brilliant glistening wood produce a strong design statement.

Warm color tones monopolize this office and work well with the deep red wood tones.

Contrasting wood shades are an
important design element in this
elegant office.

Though small in size, this office is large in
functionality. A wrap around desk surface
creates an ample work environment.

Monochromatic in nature, blue chairs create contrast in this office.

Mauves and browns blend harmoniously within this work space.

Muted blues, browns, and burgundy create a harmonious environment in this large private office.

Detail of computer niche conveniently located next to reference materials.

Surrounded by windows, this environment is lavishly filled with traditional furniture and executive style.

Opposing page:
Powerful reddish brown hues intermingle with shades of navy in this traditionally styled office.

This opulent corner office with wondrous window views is anchored by muted tones in the marble floor, carpet and upholstered seating.

Somewhat garish in nature, the brilliant colorimetric quality of the wall art contrasts pleasingly with the otherwise dull color scheme in this magnificent office.

Blond wood tones contrast
well with substantial seating in
deep red and blue hues.

A pastel color palette on the
walls and floor blend superbly
with the lacquered desk and wall
unit in creamy neutral tones.

A narrowly shaped space is enhanced with tall plantings and landscape art creating a feeling of the great outdoors.

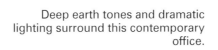

Deep earth tones and dramatic lighting surround this contemporary office.

Opposing page:
Warm light wood tones blend contiguously
with shades of peach in this desert inspired
environment.

Neutral grays are a pleasing
color choice in this open plan
office space.

Glistening sunshine from the
massive windows highlight the
white walls and guest chairs in
this powerful corner office.

The power of light is exemplified in this modest office with comfortable shades of mauves and blues encompassing elegant light blond wood fixtures. The beauty of nature is appreciated through the substantial windows creating a pleasing focal point in this view.

Opposing page:
A hand loomed vintage carpet anchors the bright white seats in this light and airy environment. The large decorative wall art solidifies the design by repeating the predominant square and rectangular shapes of the windows, skylight, carpet and upholstered furniture.

Shades of white in the wall, chairs and accent pieces contrast strongly with the mauve carpet and lush plants in this modest yet elegant design.

The highly polished lacquer desk is a focal point in this dramatic office. A feeling of mystery and suspense are created by the subdued light and color palette.

Large windows sport fetching views in this large private office. Pale earth tones create a relaxed feeling blending comfortably with the natural outdoors.

Sleek, sharp design elements of the extravagant wood wall coverings, decorative wall art, and sculptures produce continuity in this large, dramatic office.

The gorgeous black and white checker board floor in highly polished marble creates a festive entrance to this snappy high tech office. Strong contrasts of black and white and brilliant crimson produce an extremely dramatic environment.

Strong color values of red and blue intertwine with deep rich cherry wood in this contemporary mid-sized office. The gleaming chrome column adds additional glitz to this modern design.

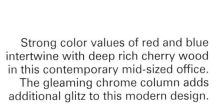

A massive curving wall of wood creates elegant movement in this open floor plan office environment. Sculptural cut outs in the wall partitions produce an artistic view with form and function while the sea of blue carpet gently caresses the entire space.

Slate floors on one side, carpet on the other, a strong contrast in textures and surfaces adds continued creative interest in this expansive floor plan.

Organic shapes blend with artistic surfaces and textures to form this modern office oasis.

Chapter 3

Board Rooms and Conference Rooms

Complex angular structures dominate this unique high rise environment. Pastel blues and pinks are contrasted by the boldly gilt framed artwork on the far wall. Natural sunlight emerges through the angled windows adding natural ambiance to this stellar space.

The bold hyoid shaped conference table, which comfortably seats twenty, majestically stands alone in this extraordinary multi-angular room. The slanting planar surface of windows produces heightened drama to the landscapes several stories below.

Photographed at night, this conference room still maintains a high level of drama with cove lighting above the table and custom designed draperies to provide privacy and comfort.

A circular table of beautiful hard wood dominates this contemporary room. Soft, delicate greenery sharply contrasts this contemporary angular space of muted colors of cream, blue, and mauve.

A built in projection screen adds a professional touch to this stately board room.

The unique shape of this conference table is mirrored in the ceiling cove above. Surfaces of the black leather chairs and highly polished wood table create visual interest in a neutrally colored space.

Decorative dome shaped lights reflect consecutive circles of light upon this ultra shiny granite table top. Blood red chairs make the room pop with color as the neutral floor and wood paneled walls maintain harmony with the beige ceiling and table surfaces.

Opposing page:
This extravagant u-shaped table seats twenty four beneath beautiful brass chandeliers. The wood ceiling beams and built in wall cabinets mimic a private home rather than a corporate space. An elegantly appointed Oriental carpet completes the décor.

A wall of glass adds comfort to this conference room as beautiful wall art can be seen in the hallway above a functional credenza. Blue colored glass panes in rectangular shapes produce a decorative and interesting design element. Detailed red diamond shapes in the ebony tabletop compliment the red chairs and draw one's eye to the brilliant crimson in the painting.

Bold vermilion chairs surround a large rectangular table and play off the black and white artwork above a black table. Fashion is depicted in the art as well as the room.

Almost iridescent in hue, these scarlet chairs are a loud statement in this ebony and white corner conference room.

Subtle lighting and neutral beige wall and floor treatments produce a powerful, yet comforting conference area.

Opposing page:
Traditional in elements and design, this large rectangular conference table provides beauty and function. A tranquil landscape painting adorns the modest wall surrounded by spacious windows in this upper floor power room.

A luxurious sea of highly polished granite adorns this majestic table that seats sixteen within a high rise conference room overlooking magnificent cityscapes.

Contemporary glitz creates an attention getting environment with highly polished surfaces and black and neutral tones with accents of copper and brass elements.

Gray leather chairs compliment the gray carpet accents in this spacious conference room.

A large frosted glass wall provides additional lighting sources to this rectangular space. The wall art enhances the room with a powerful color statement amidst an otherwise neutral hues environment.

The power of gray hues engulf this elegant and stately conference room. The shimmering granite tabletop reflects the powerful wall art of monochromatic splendor. Domed chandeliers produce warm lighting beneath the decorative ceiling cove.

Rich cherry wood wall treatments and table create a subdued powerful environment in this conference room. The wall of mirrors produces the illusion of yet more space with a touch of glitz in this expansive room.

The elegance of the Orient screams
out in this exquisite space. Priceless art
blends gracefully within the soft earth
tone hue of the walls and luxurious
plush carpet. Butter soft leather chairs
surrounding the gleaming wood table
complete the décor.

Black and white design elements flourish within this highly contemporary design. Stunning wall art boldly stands transfixed upon the far wall. An intriguing glass table of ample proportion completes the overall ambiance.

Deep hued blue-green chairs add a touch of decorative color in this neutral yet powerful office space.

Frosted window glass panes within an interior corner wall conference room create an illusion of spaciousness. A tall ceiling and light colored walls add an airy feeling in this narrow rectangular space.

Opposing page:
Magnificent elements of the Orient enliven this immense conference room of powerful proportions. Twenty-six plush leather seats encompass this beautifully polished table with gleaming brass accents. The decorative lighted ceiling cove mirrors the elegant table in size and dimension. The priceless wood details above the desk and around the ceiling and windows compliment the wood furniture with creative precision and grace.

A green marble floor design borders this deep wood toned conference room. This predominant splash of color within a richly earth-toned space of neutrals compliments the green glass rims of the overhead lighting fixtures.

A feeling of the great southwest desert comes alive in turquoise and terracotta color in this ample conference room with seating for eighteen around an exquisite wood table. A long wall of glass, which includes the entrance doors, permits a view of the delightful and artistic wall art indicative of Native American design elements.

Deep navy hues embellish this powerful but understated design. Three large wall paintings add visual interest to a neutral backdrop.

Twenty-four plush velvet chairs in royal purple command center stage in this opulent conference room. The large oval table is professionally crafted in rare burled wood and is mirrored above by a decorative and light enhanced ceiling cove. Clear glass block adds texture to the smooth white walls while colorful wall art creates a beautiful contrast.

Opposing page:
A center marble insert highlights the rich dark wood in this large square table. The blue chairs and green foliage add a soft touch to this strongly stated interior design.

Shades of turquoise enliven this angular conference room. A decorative glass wall adds texture and creativity to the smooth surfaces surrounding this space. The hexagonal ceiling design creates drama with shape, color and light.

An expansive blue gray carpet with a cream and mauve border blends color delicately in this conference room. The angled placement of the table produces pleasant movement and a feeling of yet greater space in an ample sized area.

Electric blue chairs, wall panels and carpeting dominate this powerfully hued conference room. Decorative wall art in complimentary colors flank the exterior wooden doors of the corporate presentation board.

Opposing page:
A unique rhythm of movement exists in this conference room with curving walls. Outwardly curved triangular sides of this modernistic blond wood table design produce additional activity. Groupings of small sized artwork produce an interesting pattern on the neutral gray wall. Creative floor panels lead asymmetrically to the table forming an added dramatic element.

Neutral beiges and gray capture a sense of stability in this large rectangular conference room. The huge granite topped table is the focal point of eighteen plush leather chairs within the contemporary design.

The serenity of blue shades enrobe this conference room. A large wooden wall unit provides library access while the wall art brings a feel of the southwest.

Deep coral chairs with delicate texture contrast brilliantly with the aubergine carpet and eggplant colored perimeter seating. Bursting with color, this room exemplifies strength and dominance in design.

The parabolic table packs a powerful design punch in highly polished deep cherry wood while contrasting the neutral walls and floor colorings. Shape and texture elements create a successfully dramatic affect.

An intricate and visually stimulating carpet pattern swirls around the vast table setting in this traditionally inspired conference room. Crystal chandeliers and sparkling wall sconces enhance the elegant ambiance.

A detail view of the elegant wall cabinet depicts the comfort of home within an elegant corporate conference room.

Bullet shaped legs adorn this contemporary wood table prominently placed in this contemporary board room. A sleek modern design is reinforced with an adjustable wood panel exposing a light board to view x-rays.

Lacquered pitch black table and chairs produce a striking design in this contemporary conference room dominated by hues in black and white. The trio of wall art in deep black and muted shades contrasts the long white wall.

Beautiful wood hues are the predominant factor within this moderate sized board room. The unique wooden floor design adds a patterned interest to the smooth surfaces and organic shapes of the table, chairs, and greenery.

Beige walls and flooring are complimented by deep brownish earth tones in this large masterful conference room. Chair coverings in pale hues add a delicate balance of color to the room.

Opposing page:
This octagonal room is enhanced with dramatic hues of crisp coral chairs and scarlet floor accents. Light gray and white walls with large windows form a contemporary backdrop for the colorful chairs and the glistening marble tabletop.

Earth tones decorate this modest sized conference room producing warmth and comfort in a corporate environment.

Stream lined, energy efficient lighting illuminates this inspirational conference room. The accent wall in a muted mustard hue harmonizes with the plants and flowers visible in the space. Tall narrow windows in the outward curving wall create an added dimension to this professional environment.

Monochromatic earth tones set the stage for this rectangular board room with ample overhead lighting and added interest from a wall of glass.

A variety of gray hues cover the walls, floor, and chairs in this high rise corporate conference room. Brown wood accents contrast well with the gray and compliment the natural greenery and wall art.

A majestic, seven sided conference table seats twenty-two in this extravagant conference room. Brilliant turquoise carpet and chairs vie strongly for dominance in this extraordinary design. Angled walls and a masterful ceiling cove with classic lighting complete the powerful design statement.

This detail enhances the repetition of rectangular shaped design elements present in the tabletop, wall relief, podium, table sides, and multi-media wall screens. Brilliant turquoise contrasts pleasingly with the neutral walls and ceiling.

Burgundy and mauve leather chairs surround an elegant marble topped table in this large corporate board room. Pale gray walls encircle the modern design while natural greenery adds the feeling of nature's outdoor elements.

Creamy beiges and muted tan hues create a visual backdrop for powerful blue-green chairs in this rectangular conference room. A pleasing pattern of artwork adorns the expansive wall while a symmetrical wall unit forms a solid focal point.

Fourteen cushioned seats surround this gleaming conference table befitting a king or queen. Domed ceiling lights cast a warm glow in the law firm's predominant boardroom, which houses a complete wall of reference materials.

Opopsing page:
Elements of art deco design ring out in this conference room. Earth tones and soft surfaces create an inviting atmosphere.

Beige walls commingle with muted earth tones producing a serene work environment in this moderate sized board room.

Opposing page:
A richly textured carpet produces a pleasing contrast to the smooth surfaces of the leather chairs and highly polished executive conference table. Long and sleek, this large rectangular conference room is illuminated by a combination of natural sunlight, ceiling fixtures and radiant light from the adjoining hallway through the frosted glass wall. This room boasts seating for twenty with modern comfort.

The delicate curve to this table is inherent to the contemporary design of this corporate conference room. Walls, chairs, floor, ceiling, and fixtures are covered in nature's bountiful earth tones, while the artwork accentuates a feeling of continuity within the room.